Coffee Shop Conversations
Plugged In

By: Christopher Kelly

The media we call social is an illusion with personal information that only includes the best of us, but leaves out the emotion, and the truth.

We post our experiences, purchases, and travels but in reality no one cares. We send group messages to family and friends thinking we are good at communicating when in reality we are lonely and disconnected.

Why not read a book, paint a picture, put your phone down, exercise, and look into someone's eyes. When you are in public and feel alone lift your head and put away your phone.

Why do you constantly look at your contact list when we can't even coexist with others?

Go outside if you need to talk on the phone, and please put it away if you're standing in line ordering food or coffee.

A healthy hello to the person beside you or to the many people that work in the service industry will go a long way. We don't want to hear your conversations, or how much money you make.

Put down your phone and join a friend for a cup of coffee and conversation. Kids are losing the basic skill of communication because all of their back and forth is digital. No one is learning.

Job interviews are stressful now, but they will be unbearably nerve racking when you've never looked up from your phone and carried on a conversation with another eye to eye adult.

Dating, shopping, conversing and studying are all done online now with group chat replacing looking another person in the eye, shaking their hand, having a conversation, or a hug.

How many times do you see other people texting and driving, walking, jogging, riding a bike and texting, having dinner with the family and texting, texting on the toilet, texting in the shower, texting in the middle of the night, it never ends.

Children are given IPads and IPhones with parents in the play parks disconnected on their phones with eyes that don't come off the ground.

We are a generation of smart phones and dumb people

We allow the disillusion of social media to take over our lives. In reality, no one cares about your puppy picture, your self-portrait, vacations, and all of the food shots of your meal.

Do you realize how ridiculous you look with your arm extended with phone in hand everywhere you go bumping into your neighbor. Look up dummy.

Make sure you give life the attention you deserve and you will be glad that you did. Why waste the few day, weeks, months, years left in your very short existence looking down at your screen.

Don't fool yourself and think that you're learning something new or gaining knowledge by posting comments, pictures and wasting time trying to get a like, or attention from the many on line idiots.

In reality social media is dumbing us down with useless information and posts that no one cares about or takes the time to look at.

We spend many hours together without eye contact. Look up from your phone, shut down the display, and decide to live a better life today.

Education has failed, parents have failed, our open boarders have failed, let's make your life great again before It's too late, and look up.

We are a group of ignorant animals that have evolved into savages with I-Phones. No longer do we need spears to fight back, but now can wear our pants on the ground; complain life is unfair while destroying neighborhoods and business with rocks and posting hate speech from you chair.

Technology, internet and the information we gather from it must be used and understood with an open mind. If all you do is flip through fake news and dumb posts by ignorant individuals then you become one of the dummies. Just unplug.

Coffee Shop Conversations

It tends to be a trend in coffee shops everywhere you turn people in well to do areas are pretending to use their education as a crutch to hang out like the homeless, equipped with a Mac, mocha latte, wearing t-shirts, and flip flops.

They utilize their time by complaining about the neighbors, the rude drivers, while interjecting a "like" every 3rd word. "Like" you know what I am "Like" saying, with an Ivy League degree.

It is clear to me that most have wasted their education and are living in a world of fantasy, failed businesses and personal relationships.

A well scripted presentation with terminology learned from an expensive Ivey league university while trying to convince the person to join their multi-level marketing scam seems to be a common thread in one way conversations.

It becomes apparent that our educational system has failed. It may be time for these individuals to look up, get a real job, and put down the phone.

In the end it is your choice to work or fail.

Some of the tech savvy individuals will post a go fund me page. People just like getting paid for doing nothing, and acting like a victim.

Coffee Shop Conversations

Head down, IPhone, flipping through screen after screen, standing, shuffling walking with head down, people are around her, but does not notice, she is in a fog, she has no awareness of her surroundings, or does she care.

Coffee Shop Conversations

I noticed flip flop wearing, t-shirt, shorts, backwards hat, unshaven speaking on a conference call with no respect to anyone else in close proximity of his obnoxiousness.

This late 20s person using all his business terminology from his Ivey league education to feel important sitting at a coffee shop.

His eyes glaze over looking through everyone else engaged in meaning less business conversation as if he is a CEO of a large corporation.

This is what our future graduates are doing speaking in business terms when really it is just another lemonade stand. Just squeeze the lemon.

Coffee Shop Conversations

Two girls early 30s talking and recreating step by step accounts of other people and how they act. Showing pictures and calling another girl on video phone volume turned up. They flip their hair, say like a million times, and leave me in total exhaustion listening to this crap. They continue to waste the day talking about other people.

Coffee Shop Conversations

The same person that I have seen at several coffee shops, tells his story of traveling around the world for work, but then ignores you while plugged in walking talking, in essence oblivious to anyone around him, but when he is ready likes to tell us about his travels he becomes a chatty idiot.

Coffee Shop Conversations

Customer walks in, stands at the side counter talking on phone looking through barristers just 3 feet away, and speaking loud enough for me to hear it 20 feet away – Really ?

Coffee Shop Conversations

Well to do home owner was over whelmed that she had to cut her small yard in the heat. She is normally inside with the air conditioning.

During a coffee shop job interview she talked about how hard of a worker she is with corporate management, speaking of why everyone else was a problem, but then they let her go from her job.

She stated that he work load was down, passed her 90 days probations, and they let her go.

Spoke about how others did not know how to do their jobs. I was heartbroken from being let go at my last job before this recent termination, highest salary there, but they let me go.

She never stopped talking and babbling step by step stories of this person and that person, while being interviewed at the coffee shop.

Desperation was in her voice with each minute getting further away from a job offer, she then said I'm a type A person.

After 20 minutes into the exhausting conversation she said I need to be around 85k to 90k a year.

The man never got a word in. 30 minutes later I could not take it anymore of the torture and left.

Coffee Shop Conversations

Somewhat quiet with every table taken by studious people, polite, calm, jazz music in the background. Then a couple sits next to me and the wife begins to go through the daily news and reads it out loud to her husband, yet another I-Phone use for seasoned and mature adults.

The husband sat in a slump of torture.

Coffee Shop Conversations

2 ladies sit at a small table just feet away from each other, each on their phone conversation ignoring the other talking head down disengaged in the natural world. The rest of the group with laptops out, head down. This is our future.

Coffee Shop Conversations

The drive through is busy, bumper to bumper, but every person head down on their phone. The dog is in the back seat wondering why the owner was so excited in going for a ride, but is ignoring the pet. Wait until Goggle comes out with a doggie IPad. Inside the coffee shop same experience with everyone all ages arm extended head down.

Kids have an I-Phone, parents are not parenting.

Coffee Shop Conversations

Just noticing the spring break girls in from college they are all over weight, some with tattoos, all hands out with the I phone. They ordered sugary drinks, and cakes also with the fat mama getting her share of snacks, and also on her phone.

No one was looking up from their virtual world.

Coffee Shop Conversations

3 girls, in low 20s all have their phones out, one keeps talking about someone else, telling the whole story of he said, she said, repeating someone else's past history.

This is a story we really don't want to hear, or do the other two friends pretending to listen looking up periodically from scrolling on their IPhones while she is amped up on caffeine, and continues to be annoying to the others around the table.

She was talking about running a race, when she is the fat one in the group. She ordered a salad, ate with her mouth open, and she was still talking while the other 2 are trying to get away in the car.

Coffee Shop Conversations

Amazing day the weather is perfect and the coffee shop is full of people with phones, laptops, and I pads, all missing out on the reality of nature.

Maintaining heads down into choosing a virtual reality over the surroundings with their fat kids sunk into the comfy chair, on their I-phones, drooling, sipping their sugary drinks and eating prepackage unhealthy snacks dripping in sugar.

Coffee Shop Conversations

All ages, young, old, stuck on the internet. It is a shame. Most of the adults are trying to pretend that they are in conversations with each other but can't put down the phone, and look up.

Some adults are literally just ignoring each other while sitting together, and standing with head down, pretending to be together as a group.

One woman out of the bunch has two devices going at the same time. They are all overweight of course, but don't seem to care as they eat and drink more of the crap that made them fat.

Coffee Shop Conversations

Students have a phone, laptop, and books out but most are flipping through the phone with social media with both thumbs working fast to get out a worthless text to their on line group of dummies.

This is a waste of time and life. It gives our young students the impression that they are going to be successful. In reality it's the parents fault, but then they too are on the internet ignoring reality.

Monkey see monkey do.

Coffee Shop Conversations

Obnoxious people jacked up on caffeine seem to be the norm for when you are just trying to enjoy your coffee. They spot you like radar sitting beside you when the whole place is empty. They got to come over, invade your space and destroy any hope for relaxation and peace. Then you have the parents that think the area is play time for their little angels grabbing every food item off the shelves they can get their little grubby hands on. Aren't they so sweet the parents say. Take them back to the playground please, or get a baby sitter.

Coffee Shop Conversations

You could not help listening in on a conversation coming from the drive through. It was a well to do woman in a hurry and of course her drink was not up to her expectations. She parked her car and came inside with her little kick me dog in her arm. She taped her expensive manicured fingernails on the counter demanding that her drink be redone, and to make it quick because she was in a hurry. Everyone here wanted to be rude back to her, but they just took it and moved on. This is a prime example of a stay at home wife that should have remained at home annoying her husband.

Coffee Shop Conversations

After school the coffee shop is overwhelmed by kids with 10 and 20 dollar bills. They order sugar filled specialty drinks and snacks, and then bounce off the walls jumping and screaming like an uncontrolled day care. You learn to leave before the chaos begins. This is our future.

Coffee Shop Conversations

What a great place for the homeless to hang out all day. They don't purchase anything and stink up the business environment. Sure we should do something to help them, but let's not put the responsibility on the paying customers.

Coffee Shop Conversations

When it come to the topic of religion the coffee shop should not become the new mobile church for kids and adults. I rather not have to listen to the sermons that these individuals think we all need to hear about burning in hell.

Please take the Holy Book outside, not here, not over there, not anywhere, but back into your own house to learn about the creator of the entire universe. Take time to learn about evolution.

Coffee Shop Conversations

Be on the lookout for perverts that enjoy taking pictures of individuals that are unaware that some weirdo is using his phone under the table. The dumb criminal forgot to turn off his flash, and ultimately got caught and arrested.

Coffee Shop Conversations

Please respect the baristas that serve you. They really don't want to hear about all the money you make. Remember these hard working individuals are trying to make it in this world and get paid very little to listen to your pretend success stories and embellishment of your life.

If your standing at the counter, look up from your phone, show respect, smile and be polite.

Personally I would spit in your coffee if your rude to me, but you would not notice because your too involved in the virtual world on your tiny phone. Tiny phone equals tiny hands.

The alarming statistics of reality the smart phone, digital dimensions, social media, virtual reality is dumbing us down, and mental issues are created.

We are losing the ability to memorize just one digital number, license, social security card.

Your brain is like your muscles if not used they will atrophy. If you gave your phone to a friend within 30 seconds your stress level will double.

When you take your phone out when with others, you express to them they are not important enough to put it away.

During a get together or a meeting at work once you place the phone on the table your addicted to technology. It does not matter if you put the screen side down, you're not engaged.

Parents have to intervene, but they too need to put down the phone. They are children, you can take it away. They come to 2nd grade with a phone.

The reason you don't succeed in life, is because you're not in life, or part of life.

Being in a virtual world is not living life in the real world. Don't waste away, get out and live. The guarantee of success does not exist in the real world. You have to work for it and a good start is to put down the phone, and look up.

We are good at putting filters on our social media interactions, selfies, pretending to be something you're not. A life of pretend and loneliness.

Your life is full of fakers, liars, and cheaters. Don't fall for this, look up and get out.

Posing in front of new cars, motorcycles, beaches, vacations, that most of us know you're not really into any of this pretend lifestyle. Deep meaningful relationships are not part of the new technology.

The likes, the feedback from social media becomes unbalanced when you spend more time in the world of technology, you have an addiction.

Failed parenting strategies include, you can have anything, your special, and everyone get a participation medal.

The reality is that you get nothing for coming in last. Like, like, like you know what I'm saying.

Hu, what did you say? I was not listening.

The respect that you get from a higher position in life is not the respect for a person. We have it backwards. People should respect people.

The reality is that people around us are respecting the position not the person. Do not disrespect people because of your title or position in life, and to have humility and respect for others. Just look up and speak to someone.

Top 10 Baristas Dislikes

1. You provide the spelling of your name.
2. You order with Attitude.
3. You stare at them making the drink.
4. Leaving speaker without ending your order.
5. You're on your phone during your order
6. You pour hot coffee in the trashcan.
7. You don't say the size of your drink.
8. You blame them for the prices.
9. You reply to their greeting with your order.
10. You try to scam happy hour and freebies.

The Trespasser Coffee Worker

These people camp out at a coffee shop all day, grouping tables to house his multiple laptops, various folios, and office files. He spends the rest of the day pacing the room on conference calls, meeting clients, and asking you to reset the router. Expect an invitation to his pyramid scheme in place of an actual tip. This sounds like another business scam. Quick time is running out, sign up now just give me $500 for your first payment.

The Den Mother

She's the stressed-out neighborhood mom who's taken on the dubious task of shuttling a van of youngsters to and from dance practice or theater group sing-alongs or whatever the hell it is kids do these days. Like a swarm of locusts with Kool Aid mustaches, the kids are gone as quickly as they arrived, leaving a trail of croissant crumbs, spilled milk, and food containers, pizza boxes from another fast food restaurant.

The Urbanized Customer
They come in with tattoos, man purse, yoga pants, unshaven, order a Latte for pick up with seven additional modifications and then tell everyone that they are a triathlon athlete.

Life Is Good
The middle-aged regular who's coping with early retirement by wearing nothing but sandals and a T-shirt. He adheres to a tightly regimented daily routine to show up at your coffee shop at 6:00 am, same order, and speaks about the old days.

Not Sure what I want
This person has had plenty of time to understand the menu and should be ready once they step up to the counter. They are not paying attention when you greet him. He inches closer to the register as you walk away to get some side work done, then another question about what is in the latte special.

I'm in a Hurry
This guy always ends up in line behind a regular who loves to talk the crap, and he's always super pissed. It's never clear why he's in such a hurry or so inpatient, then he spills coffee on his shirt.

The Bewildered Geriatric

It's hard enough for them to even walk into your establishment, and now you're in their face with these questions about for here or to go, what do you want, with or without, and what size?

The Scavenger

Instead of ordering something, they sneak in to rummage through the used newspapers, ask you to hold a week's worth of spent espresso for their garden, or dig through the lost & found bin for a flip-phone charger and an umbrella.

The Overbearing Dog Parent

Your dog is tiny enough to carry inside, which means it's all good, right? Not only is this wrong, but you're also creating a scenario where your dog is even closer to food products in the instance that it abruptly shits all over the place. They may look the other way at Home Depot, but not here. You're dog lover and that's great. Leave Fido in the car please.

The Shoeless Guy

Someone left this guy in your neighborhood on the way to Burning Man festival and now he can't remember which way home is. He sometimes pays for stuff, but normally just ask for a water. He sits outside and plays his banjo.

The Cyclist

He just cycled around the neighborhood with his expensive Italian carbon-fiber bicycle, brings it into the store, and pays with crumpled bills from a pocket far too close to this guy's sweat crack. We all know you live around the corner.

The Power Lunch

This macho business-type insists on having high-octane pow wows in public spaces so he can show off his snazzy new suit and matching belt clip for his iPhone. No one cares.

The Picnicker

While we certainly love cleaning up the huge lunch your mom appears to have packed for you, maybe you should order something except free water while you have your picnic at the best table inside for paying customers.

A Story from a Master Brewer

The chaos looks like a swarm of angered bees. People are maneuvering around each other in what seems like an organized tango, all the while never seeming to be in the other's way.

The sounds and smells are intoxicating, quickly followed by the shouts of orders and needed necessities for success.

As I approach my station, I am guarded with my battle gear. I take a deep breath, arm myself for the person approaching, and ready my person for the insanity inevitably headed my way.

My customer heads toward me, smiling with delight at my apparent misery. I attempt to force a smile on my lips, and prepare to do as I have been trained. I open my mouth, and utter the words,

Welcome! What can I get started for you today?

The customer seems in an annoyingly pleasant mood. Her goofy smile, gracefully accented by her long, blonde hair. Just happy to see a friend.

She appears to be in her late teens or early twenties, which immediately instills the notion that she is going to want some sort of frozen dessert-like beverage with many extras.

She looks at the menu, no doubt intimidated by the options she has to choose from, looking inquisitive as she scans over the boards.

She looks at me with her hazel eyes and says.

Is there a way to make a Frappuccino, like, healthy? I try to hide my humor at her request.

I smile and say, Well, we can make it light, which is one third fewer calories, but the Frappuccino is more of a dessert than an actual sophisticated coffee drink of which has more sugar in it.

We could make you a skinny latte, which is made with sugar-free syrup and nonfat milk. She looks at me confused, as if I had just given her the mathematical equation to understanding the way the universe works.

She sighs and says, well, I want something with whipped cream, but you just asked for something healthy, right?

Yeah, but, like, if I get something that is, like, kind of healthy, like I do not feel as bad, like, getting the whipped cream, like you know.

I deal with customers "like" her all day, wanting to find some sort of way to make something that is intentionally made to be a sweet treat into a drink that their yoga instructor would approve of.

I muster up the strength to retort something that makes sense to her, and say, we can make the Frappuccino light, which is made with nonfat milk, use a sugar-free syrup, and still add the whipped cream.

That sounds great! I will take a large.

Okay, so that is a venti sugar-free caramel Frappuccino light with whipped cream. Uh, no, I asked for a large - a venti is a large, ma'am.

Oh. I do not know coffee speak. It is confusing. Okay. Anything else? Make sure the caramel sauce is on top. I want to add that. It is delicious.

I put the order into our system, tell her the total cost for her beverage, gather her money, hand her change, and she goes about her way.

I deal with this insanity more often than I wish I did. Customers come in day after day, minute after minute, asking for things that make absolutely no sense, thinking they are the caffeine gods and this coffee shop is their Olympus.

I get the occasional customer that actually knows a thing or two about coffee.

Nothing like a master, but people who appreciate coffee in its truest sense.

But, more often than not, I get teenagers who demand their saucy, sweet blended beverages and the older customers that get irritated at the amount of foam on their espresso macchiato.

Either way, I accept the fact that I very rarely win the argument, and I just smile and let them go about their way. In the end it is about customer service and the baristas are there to make it happen providing a great environment for coffee, conversation, and internet, for all ages.

Come back often – we do sincerely miss you, and the stories of your life - Enjoy every day.

Coffee!
You can sleep when you're dead!

WHO WANTS COFFEE?

I WILL DRINK COFFEE HERE OR THERE I WILL DRINK COFFEE EVERYWHERE

I WANT COFFEE
RIGHT MEOW

COFFEE TIME

Good Morning
By Daniel
Red, White & Brew

www.ingramcontent.com/pod-product-compliance
Lightning Source LLC
Chambersburg PA
CBHW021150260726
48656CB00025B/2340